Title: 35
"STOCK SURGE:

A Blueprint for Prosperity in the American Market"

In the culmination of this enlightening journey through the realms of finance, innovation, and humanity, I extend a resounding call to action. As readers, you now hold the keys to a treasury of knowledge that transcends the conventional boundaries of financial understanding. The wisdom distilled from historical narratives, the illumination provided by cutting-edge innovations, and the profound significance of human values collectively pave the way for transformative action.It is not merely an invitation but a mandate to embrace continuous learning. Stay attuned to the pulse of evolving financial landscapes, technological breakthroughs, and ethical considerations. Let this book be your compass, guiding you through the intricate currents of a dynamic world.Embrace a human-centric approach to finance, incorporating emotional intelligence, ethical principles, and sustainable practices into your decision-making. Recognize the potential for your choices to reverberate beyond personal success, influencing the well-being of communities and contributing to a more equitable global future.As you close the final chapter, let it resonate as a catalyst for positive change. Forge a visionary path that harmonises the wisdom of tradition, the dynamism of innovation, and the enduring values of humanity. Your actions today shape the financial landscapes of tomorrow—may they be marked by integrity, foresight, and a commitment to building a brighter and more inclusive financial future.

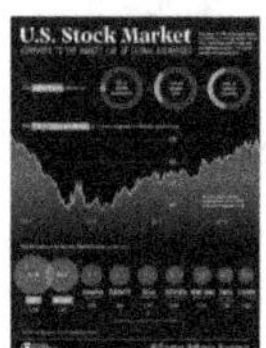

INTRODUCTION

In the dynamic world of finance, where opportunities and risks intersect, "Stock Surge: A Blueprint for Prosperity in the American Market" serves as your navigational guide. Authored by the experienced Marion S. Jones, this comprehensive handbook is designed for both novice investors seeking to unravel the intricacies of the stock market and seasoned traders aiming to enhance their strategies.Within these pages, we embark on a journey through the fundamental principles of investing, decoding market trends, and mastering the art of strategic decision-making. As we delve into the chapters that follow, Marion S. Jones shares invaluable insights garnered from years of navigating the ever-evolving landscape of the American stock market.Prepare to unlock the secrets of successful stock investing, armed with a blueprint that not only demystifies the complexities of the market but also instils the discipline required for sustained financial growth. Whether you're a newcomer or a seasoned investor, the wisdom contained herein will empower you to ride the waves of prosperity with confidence.Welcome to "Stock Surge," where the path to financial success begins.

CONTENT
*Introduction to the stock market
*Strategic Investing Foundations
*Stock Selection strategies
*Timing the Market
*Risk Management
*Winning Portfolios
*Market Psychology mastery
*Leveraging Technology
*Advanced Trading Strategies
*Continuous Learning
*Real-life Case Studies
*Conclusion: Prosperity Awaits

Chapter 1: INTRODUCTION TO THE STOCK MARKET: Basics of the Stock Market**Welcome to the fascinating world of the stock market—a realm where financial opportunities unfold and fortunes are shaped. In this chapter, we embark on a journey to demystify the fundamentals, providing you with the essential knowledge to navigate the complexities of stock trading.**

UNRAVELLING THE MARKET FABRIC:**At its core, the stock market is a dynamic marketplace where buyers and sellers converge to trade shares of publicly listed companies. These companies, often referred to as "stocks" or "equities," represent ownership in a portion of the business. Understanding this foundational concept is crucial as we navigate the upcoming chapters.**

THE IMPORTANCE OF INVESTING INVESTING: **in the stock market goes beyond merely buying and selling shares—it's a strategic approach to growing wealth over time. Whether you're an aspiring investor or a seasoned trader, recognizing the significance of putting your money to work in the market is the first step towards financial success.**

THE JOURNEY BEGINS:**Our journey begins with the exploration of basic stock market terminology and concepts. From understanding how stocks are traded to grasping the significance of market indices, this chapter lays the groundwork for your venture into the captivating world of stock investing.**

KEY TERMS AND CONCEPTS:**Before we dive into the intricacies of strategic investing, let's familiarise ourselves with key terms such as "bull market" and "bear market," and concepts like "dividends" and "market capitalization." These building blocks will serve as the foundation for your stock market education.**

YOUR INVESTMENT BLUEPRINT:**As we progress, envision your investment journey as a blueprint—a personalised guide that evolves with your financial goals and risk tolerance. The stock market is not a one-size-fits-all endeavour; your approach should align with your unique circumstances and aspirations.As we conclude this chapter, armed with newfound knowledge, you're well-equipped to navigate the stock market with** confidence. The subsequent chapters will delve deeper into strategic investing principles, empowering you to make informed decisions and set the stage for a prosperous financial future

CHAPTER 2: STRATEGIC INVESTING FOUNDATIONS

FUNDAMENTAL ANALYSIS:**In the intricate dance of the stock market, understanding the fundamentals of the companies you invest in is paramount. Fundamental analysis involves evaluating a company's financial health, management, competitive position, and growth prospects. It's the cornerstone of informed decision-making in the stock market.**

UNVEILING FINANCIAL HEALTH:
Examining a company's financial statements—balance sheet, income statement, and cash flow statement—provides a snapshot of its financial health. Key metrics like revenue growth, profitability, and debt levels offer crucial insights into the company's stability and potential for future growth.

MANAGEMENT MATTERS:**Beyond financials, evaluating a company's management is crucial. Effective leadership can steer a company through challenges and capitalise on opportunities. Investigate the track record of the management team, their strategic vision, and their ability to adapt to market dynamics.**

TECHNICAL ANALYSIS:**While fundamental analysis dives into the company's inner workings, technical analysis focuses on historical price and volume patterns to predict future market movements. Charts become your compass, guiding you through the ebbs and flows of stock prices.**

CHART PATTERNS AND TRENDS:**Technical analysts study chart patterns, recognizing trends that can indicate potential buying or selling opportunities. Whether it's a bullish uptrend signalling upward momentum or a bearish downtrend suggesting potential declines, these patterns inform your strategic decisions.**

INDICATORS AND OSCILLATORS:**Indicators and oscillators, such as moving averages and relative strength index (RSI), offer additional layers of analysis. They help identify overbought or oversold conditions, aiding in the timing of entry and exit points in the market.**

CRAFTING YOUR INVESTMENT STRATEGY:**As we navigate the waters of strategic investing, it's essential to** integrate both fundamental and technical analyses into your decision-making process. A balanced approach allows you to leverage the strengths of each method, creating a robust investment strategy tailored to your goals and risk tolerance.

BALANCING ACT:Consider fundamental and technical analyses as complementary tools rather than competing ideologies. By combining these approaches, you enhance your ability to make well-informed investment decisions and navigate the dynamic landscape of the stock market.

YOUR INVESTMENT TOOLKIT:
Armed with the knowledge gained from this chapter, you're equipped with a toolkit comprising fundamental and technical analysis. The subsequent chapters will guide you through applying these tools to real-world scenarios, empowering you to strategically navigate the stock market with confidence.

CHAPTER 3: STOCK SELECTION STRATEGIES: RESEARCHING PROMISING STOCKS:**In the vast sea of stocks, identifying promising investments requires careful research and analysis. This chapter delves into effective stock selection strategies to help you navigate the markets with confidence.**

FUNDAMENTAL RESEARCH:
EARNINGS PER SHARE (EPS): Assess a company's profitability by examining its earnings per share. Consistent growth in EPS is often a positive indicator.

PRICE-TO-EARNINGS (P/E) RATIO: Evaluate the relationship between a stock's price and its earnings. A lower P/E ratio may suggest an undervalued stock.

DIVIDEND HISTORY: For income-focused investors, analysing a company's dividend history provides insights into its commitment to returning value to shareholders.

TECHNICAL RESEARCH:
TREND ANALYSIS: Identify the prevailing trend using charts. A stock in an uptrend may present buying opportunities, while a downtrend may signal caution.

SUPPORT AND RESISTANCE LEVELS: Pinpoint levels where a stock has historically struggled (resistance) or found support. These levels can guide entry and exit points.

VOLUME ANALYSIS: Examine trading volume to gauge the strength of a price movement. Higher volume during an uptrend can signify conviction among investors.

DIVERSIFICATION PRINCIPLES:**While selecting promising stocks is crucial, equally important is the principle of diversification. Spreading your investments across different sectors and asset classes mitigates risk and enhances the stability of your portfolio.**

SECTOR DIVERSIFICATION:**Allocate your investments across various sectors such as technology, healthcare, finance, and others. This guards against downturns in any single industry impacting your entire portfolio.**

ASSET CLASS DIVERSIFICATION:**In addition to stocks, consider diversifying into other asset classes like bonds or real estate. A well-balanced portfolio provides a buffer against market volatility.**

CRAFTING YOUR INVESTMENT PORTFOLIO:**With a wealth of information on stock selection and diversification, it's time to craft a winning investment portfolio. This involves strategically combining stocks that align with your investment goals, risk tolerance, and time horizon.Your**

PERSONALISED PORTFOLIO:**Consider the allocation of assets based on your financial objectives. Are you seeking long-term growth, income, or a combination of both? Tailor your portfolio to reflect your unique investment strategy.**

MONITORING AND ADJUSTING:**A successful portfolio is dynamic. Regularly monitor your investments and be prepared to adjust your holdings based on changes in market conditions, economic trends, and your own financial goals.As we conclude this chapter, you've gained insights into effective stock selection strategies and the principles of diversification. The subsequent chapters will guide you further on your journey to building a robust and prosperous investment portfolio.**

CHAPTER 4: TIMING THE MARKET:
MARKET CYCLES AND

TRENDS:**Understanding market cycles and trends is instrumental in making well-timed investment decisions. In this chapter, we explore the ebb and flow of the market, helping you navigate the ever-changing landscape with precision.**

THE ART OF MARKET CYCLES:
BULL MARKETS: Discover the characteristics of bull markets, marked by rising stock prices and an optimistic investor sentiment. Learn to identify early signs and potential strategies for capitalising on upward trends.

BEAR MARKETS: **Navigate the challenges of bear markets, characterised by falling stock prices and a pessimistic outlook. Explore defensive strategies to protect your portfolio during market downturns.**

IDENTIFYING TRENDS:
TECHNICAL INDICATORS: Leverage technical indicators, such as moving averages and trendlines, to identify the prevailing direction of the market. These tools serve as invaluable guides for recognizing trends and potential reversals.

CYCLICAL AND SECULAR TRENDS: Differentiate between short-term cyclical trends and long-term secular trends. Understanding these dynamics aids in aligning your investment strategy with the broader market movements.

EFFECTIVE MARKET TIMING: **StrategiesAccurate market timing can significantly impact the success of your investments. This section explores various strategies to optimise entry and exit points, ensuring you stay ahead of market shifts.**

CONTRARIAN INVESTING:**Embrace the contrarian approach by going against prevailing market sentiment. Explore how contrarian strategies can be employed during both bull and bear markets to uncover hidden opportunities.**

DOLLAR-COST AVERAGING:**Mitigate the impact of market volatility by employing dollar-cost averaging. This disciplined approach involves regularly investing a fixed amount, regardless of market conditions, potentially reducing the impact of short-term fluctuations on your overall portfolio.**

SEASONAL TRENDS:**Recognize the impact of seasonal trends on market behaviour. Explore historical patterns and consider adjusting your investment strategy based on the time of the year to capitalise on seasonal opportunities.**

CRAFTING YOUR MARKET TIMING STRATEGY:**As we navigate the intricacies of market cycles and timing strategies, it's essential to tailor your approach to align with your risk tolerance and investment goals.**

YOUR PERSONALISED TIMING BLUEPRINT:**Consider developing a personalised timing blueprint that incorporates elements of both fundamental and technical analysis. This dynamic strategy evolves with market conditions, allowing you to adapt to the ever-changing financial landscape.**

CONSISTENCY AND DISCIPLINE:**Successful market timing requires consistency and discipline. Establish clear guidelines for entering and exiting positions, and resist the urge to succumb to emotional reactions triggered by short-term market fluctuations.In conclusion, this chapter equips you with the tools to decipher market cycles, identify trends, and implement effective timing strategies. As you embark on your journey through the subsequent chapters, you'll further refine your ability to navigate the stock market with precision and confidence.**

CHAPTER 5: RISK MANAGEMENT:
IMPORTANCE OF RISK

ASSESSMENT:In the dynamic world of stock investing, risk is an inherent companion. This chapter delves into the critical importance of risk assessment, providing you with the tools and insights needed to safeguard your investments.
RECOGNIZING DIFFERENT TYPES Of RISK:

**MARKET RISK: Understand the broader market forces that can impact the value of your investments. From economic downturns to geopolitical events, market risk requires vigilant monitoring.

COMPANY-SPECIFIC RISK: Examine risks associated with individual companies, such as poor management decisions, competitive pressures, or financial instability. A thorough analysis helps mitigate company-specific risks.

QUANTIFYING RISK TOLERANCE:
**FINANCIAL GOALS: Align your risk tolerance with your financial goals. Assess whether you're investing for long-term growth, income, or a combination of both, tailoring your risk strategy accordingly.

**TIME HORIZON: Consider your investment time horizon. Longer timeframes often allow for a higher tolerance for market fluctuations, while shorter horizons may necessitate a more conservative approach.
TOOLS AND TECHNIQUES FOR RISK MANAGEMENT:

effectively managing risk involves employing a range of tools and techniques. This section introduces practical approaches to mitigate potential pitfalls.

ASSET ALLOCATION
Distribute your investments across different asset classes to reduce the impact of a poorly performing sector or industry. A well-diversified portfolio can help maintain stability during market turbulence.

STOP-LOSS ORDERS:
Implement stop-loss orders to automatically sell a security if it reaches a predetermined price. This tool

provides a level of protection against significant losses, especially in volatile market conditions.

HEDGING STRATEGIES:
Explore hedging strategies, such as options and futures, to offset potential losses. While advanced, these techniques can provide an additional layer of protection against adverse market movements.

BALANCING RISK AND REWARD:
The key to successful investing lies in striking the right balance between risk and reward. This section guides you through the process of optimising your risk-return profile.

RISK-ADJUSTED RETURNS:
Evaluate investments not only based on potential returns but also on the level of risk involved. Assessing risk-adjusted returns ensures a more comprehensive understanding of an investment's true value.

REGULAR PORTFOLIO REASSESSMENT:As market conditions evolve, so should your risk management strategy. Regularly reassess your portfolio, adjusting your risk exposure based on changes in economic conditions, market trends, and personal circumstances.In conclusion, mastering risk management is a crucial aspect of navigating the stock market. Armed with the insights from this chapter, you're better equipped to make informed decisions that align with your risk tolerance, protecting and enhancing your investment portfolio.

CHAPTER 6: BUILDING A WINNING PORTFOLIO A
SYMPHONY Of STOCKS AND STRATEGIES UNVEILED:

CREATING A BALANCED STOCK PORTFOLIO
**Embark on a journey into the artistry of investment as we
explore the intricate process of crafting a winning
portfolio. In this chapter, we delve deep into the
symphony of stocks, guiding you through the harmonious
integration of diverse assets to orchestrate a robust and
prosperous investment portfolio.**

THE PALETTE OF POSSIBILITIES

EQUITY SELECTION: **Uncover the secrets to selecting
individual stocks that resonate with your financial goals.
We explore how to identify companies with growth
potential, income-generating capabilities, and a solid
foundation for long-term success.**

SECTORAL SYMPHONY: **Navigate the diverse sectors of
the market as if they were musical notes in a composition.
Understand the importance of sector allocation in creating
a well-balanced portfolio that thrives in varying economic
climates.**

THE ROLE OF DIFFERENT ASSET CLASSES

EQUITIES, BONDS, AND BEYOND: **Elevate your
understanding of asset classes beyond equities. Discover
the nuances of incorporating bonds, real estate, and other
investment vehicles into your portfolio, adding layers of
resilience and stability.**

RISK MITIGATION STRATEGIES: **Witness how strategic
asset allocation acts as a conductor, harmonising risk and
reward. Learn to navigate market volatility by strategically
positioning your assets to weather different financial
tempests.**

THE DANCE OF DIVERSIFICATION

GEOGRAPHICAL CHOREOGRAPHY

GLOBAL MARKET EXPOSURE: **Expand your investment
horizons beyond borders. Delve into the advantages of
international diversification, gaining insights into tapping**

into global opportunities while managing associated risks.

EMERGING MARKETS PAS DE DEUX: **Explore the dynamic dance with emerging markets. Understand the unique rhythms of investing in economies poised for growth, unveiling the potential for enhanced returns and portfolio dynamism.**

REAL-TIME PORTFOLIO MANAGEMENT

CONTINUOUS REBALANCING: **Witness the choreography of continuous rebalancing. Learn how to adjust your portfolio's composition in response to market movements, ensuring it remains in tune with your financial objectives.**

MARKET EVENTS WALTZ:
Navigate the twists and turns of market events with grace. Explore how staying attuned to economic shifts and geopolitical dynamics allows you to pivot your portfolio strategies effectively.

THE CRESCENDO OF SUCCESS
As we conclude this chapter, you'll have not only gained a comprehensive understanding of building a winning portfolio but also acquired the skills to orchestrate its success. Your personalised financial symphony awaits, composed with strategic brilliance and conducted with the wisdom to navigate the intricate rhythms of the ever-changing market.

CHAPTER 7: MASTERING MARKET PSYCHOLOGY - STRATEGIES AND Stories OF EMOTIONAL INTELLIGENCE IN INVESTING

UNRAVELLING The EMOTIONAL TAPESTRY OF INVESTING

Embark on a captivating exploration of the psychological nuances that shape market dynamics. In this chapter, we delve into the realm of market psychology, revealing strategies and real-life stories that illuminate the art of mastering emotions in the world of investing.

THE EMOTIONAL ROLLER COASTER

GREED AND FEAR DYNAMICS: **Explore the powerful interplay of greed and fear that influences market sentiment. Uncover how recognizing and managing these emotions can lead to informed decision-making.**

HERDING BEHAVIOUR: **Peer into the crowd mentality that often governs markets. Learn how understanding herd behaviour empowers you to navigate trends and identify potential contrarian opportunities.**

STRATEGIES FOR EMOTIONAL RESILIENCE

RATIONAL DECISION-MAKING
STOICISM IN INVESTING: **Draw inspiration from stoic philosophy to cultivate emotional resilience. Discover how maintaining a rational mindset during market volatility can lead to sound investment decisions.**

SYSTEMATIC INVESTING: **Embrace systematic approaches to reduce emotional bias. Explore strategies like dollar-cost averaging, allowing you to consistently invest without succumbing to the emotional turbulence of market fluctuations.**

LEARNING FROM THE MASTERS
WARREN BUFFETT'S PATIENCE: **Delve into the wisdom of Warren Buffett and his emphasis on long-term investing. Understand the power of patience in the face of short-term market fluctuations.**

PETER LYNCH'S COMMON SENSE: **Uncover the straightforward yet profound advice of Peter Lynch. Learn** how applying common sense to investment decisions can cut through emotional noise and enhance portfolio performance.

REAL-LIFE STORIES OF TRIUMPH AND TURMOIL

THE TALE OF MR. MARKET
BENJAMIN GRAHAM'S ALLEGORY: **Explore the allegory of Mr. Market as introduced by Benjamin Graham. Gain insights into the erratic nature of market prices and how a disciplined investor can capitalise on opportunities created by Mr. Market's mood swings.**

THE DOT-COM BUBBLE BURST
LESSONS FROM THE DOT-COM ERA:
Reflect on the euphoria and subsequent crash of the dot-com bubble. Extract valuable lessons on the consequences of irrational exuberance and the importance of maintaining a clear-headed approach during market manias.

NAVIGATING MARKET SENTIMENT

CONTRARIAN STRATEGIES
THE BUFFETT INDICATOR: **Analyse market valuations using the Buffett Indicator. Explore how contrarian strategies can be employed when market sentiment reaches extremes, presenting opportunities for value investors.**
BEHAVIOURAL FINANCE INSIGHTS: **Dive into behavioural finance principles that explain market anomalies. Understand how cognitive biases can impact decision-making and implement strategies to counteract these biases.**

YOUR EMOTIONAL INTELLIGENCE BLUEPRINT
As we conclude this chapter, you'll be equipped not only with a profound understanding of market psychology but also with practical strategies derived from the experiences of investment legends and real-life market scenarios. Your journey toward mastering emotional intelligence in investing awaits, offering the potential for informed decisions and enduring success in the ever-evolving financial landscape.

CHAPTER 8: LEVERAGING TECHNOLOGY IN STOCK TRADING - A DEEP DIVE INTO ANALYTICAL TOOLS AND TECHNOLOGICAL ADVANCEMENTS

THE EVOLVING LANDSCAPE OF STOCK TRADING: **Embark on an intellectual exploration into the intersection of technology and stock trading. In this chapter, we delve into the sophisticated world of analytical tools and technological advancements, unveiling the intricacies that shape modern investment strategies.**

HARNESSING BIG DATA AND ANALYTICS
QUANTITATIVE ANALYSIS: **Delve into the world of quantitative analysis, where vast datasets are dissected to identify patterns and trends. Explore how algorithms and mathematical models contribute to making data-driven investment decisions.**

MACHINE LEARNING ALGORITHMS: **Uncover the power of machine learning algorithms in predicting market movements. From pattern recognition to predictive analytics, understand how artificial intelligence is revolutionising stock trading strategies.**

ADVANCED ANALYTICAL TOOLS

TECHNICAL ANALYSIS REIMAGINED
ALGORITHMIC TRADING SYSTEMS: **Explore the realm of algorithmic trading, where computer algorithms execute trades based on predefined criteria. Investigate how these systems provide efficiency and precision in executing complex trading strategies.**

ADVANCED CHARTING PLATFORMS: **Elevate your understanding of charting platforms with advanced features. Uncover the nuances of candlestick patterns, Fibonacci retracements, and other advanced charting techniques that empower traders to make informed decisions.**

QUANTITATIVE TOOLS FOR FUNDAMENTAL ANALYSIS

FINANCIAL MODELLING: **Delve into financial modelling techniques used by analysts to evaluate a company's intrinsic value. Understand the process of forecasting** future financial performance based on historical data and industry trends.

SCENARIO ANALYSIS: **Explore the application of scenario analysis in assessing potential impacts on investments. From stress testing to understanding various economic scenarios, learn how analysts use quantitative tools to enhance decision-making.**

TECHNOLOGICAL PLATFORMS FOR STOCK TRADING

HIGH-FREQUENCY TRADING (HFT)
MICROSECOND PRECISION: **Explore the world of high-frequency trading, where trades are executed in microseconds. Analyse the strategies employed by HFT firms and their impact on market liquidity and efficiency.**

RISK MANAGEMENT IN HFT: **Understand the intricacies of risk management in high-frequency trading. Delve into how advanced algorithms monitor and manage risks in real-time to ensure the sustainability of trading strategies.**

BLOCKCHAIN AND CRYPTOCURRENCIES
DECENTRALISED FINANCE (DEFI): **Investigate the disruptive potential of blockchain and decentralised finance. Explore how smart contracts and decentralised applications are redefining traditional financial systems.**

CRYPTOCURRENCY TRADING STRATEGIES: **Analyse trading strategies in the cryptocurrency market. From trend following to arbitrage, gain insights into the unique dynamics of this emerging asset class.**

THE FUTURE OF STOCK TRADING

QUANTUM COMPUTING
QUANTUM ADVANTAGE: **Explore the potential impact of quantum computing on stock trading. Discuss how quantum algorithms could revolutionise complex calculations, transforming analytical capabilities in the financial sector.**

ETHICAL CONSIDERATIONS
ALGORITHMIC BIAS AND ETHICS: **Delve into the ethical considerations surrounding algorithmic trading. Analyse the potential biases embedded in algorithms and the**

ethical implications of technology-driven trading strategies.

CRAFTING YOUR ANALYTICAL EDGE
As we conclude this chapter, you're poised to navigate the cutting edge of stock trading technology. Armed with an intellectual understanding of advanced analytical tools and technological advancements, you have the insights to craft a strategic and informed approach in the ever-evolving landscape of financial markets.

CHAPTER 9: ADVANCED TRADING STRATEGIES -
TACTICS for SUCCESS IN THE DYNAMIC MARKETPLACE

UNVEILING ADVANCED TRADING STRATEGIES
Embark on a strategic journey into the heart of advanced trading methodologies. In this chapter, we dissect proven trading strategies and tactical manoeuvres, providing a roadmap for achieving success in the dynamic and ever-evolving landscape of the financial markets.

MOMENTUM TRADING
RIDING THE WAVE: **Explore the art of momentum trading, where traders capitalise on the continuation of existing trends. Uncover techniques for identifying and riding momentum, leveraging price trends for potential profit.**

BREAKOUT STRATEGIES: **Delve into breakout strategies, a tactical approach to trading that capitalises on the emergence of new trends. Understand how to identify key breakout points and position yourself to take advantage of significant price movements.**

TACTICAL PRECISION IN TECHNICAL ANALYSIS

FIBONACCI RETRACEMENT
GOLDEN RATIO INSIGHTS: **Gain an in-depth understanding of Fibonacci retracement levels. Explore how these mathematical ratios can be applied to identify potential support and resistance levels, adding precision to entry and exit points.**

EXTENSION PATTERNS: **Uncover the secrets of Fibonacci extension patterns. Discover how these extensions project potential future price levels, providing traders with insights into possible profit targets.**

BOLLINGER BANDS STRATEGY
VOLATILITY SIGNALS: **Explore Bollinger Bands as a tool for assessing volatility. Understand how these bands can signal potential trend reversals and identify periods of market consolidation.**

SQUEEZE PLAYS: **Investigate Bollinger Band squeeze plays, a strategy that anticipates explosive price movements following periods of low volatility. Learn how** to spot squeeze conditions and position yourself for potential breakout opportunities.

TACTICAL PRECISION IN FUNDAMENTAL ANALYSIS

EARNINGS MOMENTUM
EARNINGS SURPRISE STRATEGIES: **Examine the impact of earnings surprises on stock prices. Learn how to strategically position yourself based on companies exceeding or falling short of market expectations.**

FORWARD GUIDANCE ANALYSIS: **Uncover the significance of forward guidance in fundamental analysis. Explore how a company's guidance for future performance can influence market sentiment and drive trading decisions.**

VALUE INVESTING STRATEGIES
CONTRARIAN VALUE APPROACH: **Embrace the contrarian value approach to investing. Discover how identifying undervalued assets and patiently waiting for market sentiment to align with intrinsic value can lead to long-term success.**

DIVIDEND GROWTH INVESTING: **Explore the tactical advantages of dividend growth investing. Understand how consistent dividend payments and the potential for dividend increases contribute to a resilient and income-generating portfolio.**

ACHIEVING SUCCESS THROUGH DISCIPLINE AND RISK MANAGEMENT

TRADING PSYCHOLOGY
DISCIPLINED DECISION-MAKING: **Cultivate disciplined decision-making in the face of market fluctuations. Explore the psychological aspects of trading and strategies for maintaining a clear mindset during periods of stress.**

ADAPTIVE RISK MANAGEMENT: **Implement adaptive risk management techniques. Learn how to adjust your risk exposure based on market conditions, preserving capital and positioning yourself for sustainable success.**

CONTINUOUS LEARNING AND ADAPTATION
STAYING INFORMED: **Emphasise the importance of continuous learning in the rapidly evolving financial landscape. Explore resources and strategies for staying informed about market trends, technological advancements, and global economic shifts.**

ADAPTING TO CHANGE: **Navigate the inevitability of change in financial markets. Understand the importance of adapting your trading strategies to evolving market conditions, ensuring flexibility in the pursuit of sustained success.**

CRAFTING YOUR PATH TO TRADING MASTERY

As we conclude this chapter, you're equipped with a comprehensive toolkit of advanced trading strategies, tactical manoeuvres, and the wisdom to navigate the intricate dance of the financial markets. Your path to trading mastery awaits, paved with proven strategies and a disciplined approach, offering the potential for sustained success in the dynamic world of trading.

Chapter 10: CONTINUOUS LEARNING AND STRATEGIC
ADAPTATION - NAVIGATING THE EVER-EVOLVING
FINANCIAL LANDSCAPE

EMBRACING A CULTURE OF CONTINUOUS LEARNING
**Embark on a journey of perpetual growth and adaptation
as we delve into the importance of continuous learning in
the financial realm. In this chapter, we explore strategies
for staying informed, evolving with market trends, and
cultivating a mindset that thrives on knowledge in the
dynamic landscape of finance.**

LIFELONG LEARNING IN FINANCE
THE POWER OF KNOWLEDGE: **Uncover the
transformative potential of lifelong learning in finance.
Explore how staying informed about market dynamics,
economic shifts, and emerging technologies positions
you as a resilient and adaptive participant in the financial
arena.**

LEARNING RESOURCES: **Navigate a sea of learning
resources, from reputable financial publications and
academic journals to online courses and industry
conferences. Discover avenues that suit your learning
style and contribute to your continuous education.**

ADAPTING TO TECHNOLOGICAL INNOVATION

FINTECH REVOLUTION
FINTECH INTEGRATION: **Explore the transformative
impact of financial technology on traditional finance.
Understand how advancements in fintech, from
blockchain to robo-advisors, are reshaping investment
landscapes and presenting new opportunities.**

DATA ANALYTICS MASTERY: **Delve into the role of data
analytics in financial decision-making. Learn how to
harness the power of data-driven insights to refine
investment strategies and gain a competitive edge in the
digital era.**

THE RISE OF ARTIFICIAL INTELLIGENCE

AI in TRADING ALGORITHMS: **Examine the integration of
artificial intelligence in trading algorithms. Explore how
machine learning models and predictive analytics**

contribute to the creation of sophisticated trading strategies.

ALGORITHMIC TRADING ETHICS: **Delve into the ethical considerations surrounding algorithmic trading. Discuss the responsible use of AI in finance and the importance of aligning technological advancements with ethical standards.**

MASTERING GLOBAL ECONOMIC TRENDS

GLOBAL ECONOMIC SHOCK

IMPACT OF GLOBAL EVENTS: **Analyse the impact of global economic events on financial markets. Explore strategies for navigating economic shocks, geopolitical shifts, and pandemics, ensuring resilience in the face of unforeseen challenges.**

CRISIS MANAGEMENT: **Uncover crisis management strategies for investors. Learn from historical events and understand how strategic decision-making during crises can mitigate risks and position portfolios for recovery.**

SUSTAINABLE INVESTING
ENVIRONMENTAL, SOCIAL, AND GOVERNANCE (ESG) PRINCIPLES

ESG INTEGRATION: **Embrace the principles of environmental, social, and governance (ESG) investing. Explore how aligning investment decisions with ethical and sustainability criteria contributes to long-term financial success.**

IMPACT INVESTING: **Investigate the world of impact investing, where financial returns are coupled with positive social and environmental outcomes. Understand how conscious investment choices can shape a more sustainable and responsible financial future.**

ETHICAL CONSIDERATIONS in FINANCE

ETHICS IN FINANCIAL DECISION-MAKING: **Navigate the ethical considerations that arise in finance. Explore the principles of integrity, transparency, and accountability,** and their role in fostering trust within the financial ecosystem.

CORPORATE SOCIAL RESPONSIBILITY: **Delve into the concept of corporate social responsibility (CSR) and its impact on investment decisions. Understand how socially responsible investing contributes to a more sustainable and equitable global economy.**

CRAFTING YOUR RESILIENT FINANCIAL FUTURE

As we conclude this chapter, you're equipped with the knowledge and strategies to navigate the ever-evolving financial landscape. Embrace continuous learning, adapt to technological innovations, master global economic trends, and align your investments with ethical considerations. Your journey towards a resilient and successful financial future is marked by a commitment to growth, knowledge, and strategic adaptation.

CHAPTER 11: FUTURE FRONTIERS Of FINANCE - NAVIGATING EMERGING TRENDS AND UNCHARTED TERRITORIES

THE DAWN OF DIGITAL ASSETS

Embark on an exploration of the evolving landscape of finance as we dive into the emergence of digital assets. In this chapter, we unravel the complexities of cryptocurrencies, central bank digital currencies (CBDCs), and decentralised finance (DeFi), providing profound insights into the future of financial ecosystems.

CRYPTOCURRENCIES: BEYOND BITCOIN

RISE OF ALTCOINS: **Explore the expanding universe of cryptocurrencies beyond Bitcoin. Uncover the unique features and potential use cases of alternative digital assets, from Ethereum's smart contracts to decentralised finance tokens.**

REGULATORY CONSIDERATIONS: **Delve into the evolving regulatory landscape surrounding cryptocurrencies. Understand how regulatory frameworks are shaping the acceptance and integration of digital assets into traditional financial systems.**

DECENTRALISED FINANCE (DEFI) REVOLUTION

BUILDING BLOCKS OF DEFI

SMART CONTRACTS AND DECENTRALISED EXCHANGES: **Examine the foundational elements of decentralised finance. Understand the role of smart contracts in automating financial transactions and the emergence of decentralised exchanges reshaping how assets are traded.**

LIQUIDITY POOLS AND YIELD FARMING: **Explore advanced concepts such as liquidity pools and yield farming. Uncover how DeFi protocols incentivize users to provide liquidity and generate yields in a decentralised ecosystem.**

CHALLENGES AND OPPORTUNITIES

SECURITY CONCERNS: **Address the security challenges associated with DeFi platforms. Explore strategies for mitigating risks and ensuring the safety of assets in a decentralised financial environment.**

FINANCIAL INCLUSION: **Analyse how DeFi is reshaping the landscape of financial inclusion. Discuss the potential for decentralised finance to provide access to financial services for individuals traditionally excluded from traditional banking systems.**

CENTRAL BANK DIGITAL CURRENCIES (CBDCS)

THE EVOLUTION OF NATIONAL CURRENCIES

GOVERNMENT-BACKED DIGITAL CURRENCIES: **Explore the concept of Central Bank Digital Currencies. Understand how governments are exploring the issuance of digital versions of their national currencies and the potential implications for monetary policy.**

GLOBAL IMPACT: **Analyse the global impact of CBDCs on international trade, cross-border transactions, and the stability of the global financial system. Consider the potential for collaboration and competition among nations in the realm of digital currencies.**

ARTIFICIAL INTELLIGENCE AND QUANTUM FINANCE

REVOLUTIONISING ANALYTICAL CAPABILITIES

QUANTUM COMPUTING APPLICATIONS: **Delve into the potential applications of quantum computing in finance. Explore how quantum algorithms could revolutionise complex calculations, risk modelling, and optimization strategies.**

AI-POWERED PREDICTIVE ANALYTICS: **Analyse the role of artificial intelligence in predictive analytics. Explore how machine learning models can uncover patterns, predict market movements, and enhance decision-making for investors and financial institutions.**

THE EVOLUTION OF SUSTAINABLE FINANCE

ESG PRINCIPLES in the FINANCIAL SECTOR

GREEN FINANCE INITIATIVES: **Explore the integration of environmental, social, and governance (ESG) principles into financial decision-making. Discuss the rise of green finance initiatives and the role of finance in addressing climate change.**

IMPACT INVESTING MATURITY: **Analyse the growing maturity of impact investing. Discuss how investors are increasingly prioritising not only financial returns but also positive social and environmental outcomes in their investment decisions.**

CRAFTING YOUR PATH IN FUTURE FINANCE

As we conclude this chapter, you're equipped with a profound understanding of the future frontiers of finance. Navigate the realms of digital assets, decentralised finance, central bank digital currencies, artificial intelligence, quantum computing, and sustainable finance. Your journey towards mastering the future of finance is marked by adaptability, knowledge, and a strategic vision for the evolving financial landscape.

CHAPTER 12: THE HUMAN ELEMENT IN FINANCE - NURTURING EMOTIONAL INTELLIGENCE, ETHICS, AND SUSTAINABLE PRACTICES

CULTIVATING EMOTIONAL INTELLIGENCE in FINANCIAL DECISION-MAKING

Embark on an exploration of the crucial role of emotional intelligence in the financial world. In this chapter, we delve into the significance of self-awareness, empathy, and ethical decision-making, shedding light on how emotional intelligence contributes to success in finance.

EMOTIONAL RESILIENCE

NAVIGATING MARKET VOLATILITY: **Explore strategies for maintaining composure during market fluctuations. Learn how emotional resilience enables investors to make rational decisions and avoid impulsive actions driven by fear or greed.**

STRESS MANAGEMENT: **Uncover techniques for managing stress in the fast-paced world of finance. Understand the importance of maintaining a balanced mindset to make well-informed decisions, even in high-pressure situations.**

ETHICAL CONSIDERATIONS IN FINANCE

UPHOLDING INTEGRITY

TRANSPARENCY AND ACCOUNTABILITY: **Examine the principles of transparency and accountability in financial decision-making. Discuss how ethical behaviour fosters trust among stakeholders and contributes to the long-term sustainability of financial practices.**

CORPORATE GOVERNANCE: **Explore the role of corporate governance in maintaining ethical standards. Discuss how robust governance structures contribute to the fair and responsible management of financial organisations.**

RESPONSIBLE INVESTING

SOCIALLY RESPONSIBLE INVESTMENT (SRI): **Delve into the concept of socially responsible investing. Discuss** how investors can align their financial goals with ethical considerations, supporting businesses that prioritise environmental, social, and governance (ESG) principles.

IMPACT MEASUREMENT: **Explore methodologies for measuring the impact of investments on society and the environment. Understand how impact measurement tools contribute to the evaluation of the ethical and sustainable outcomes of investment portfolios.**

FINANCIAL EDUCATION AND INCLUSION

EMPOWERING COMMUNITIES

PROMOTING FINANCIAL LITERACY: **Analyse the importance of financial education in fostering economic empowerment. Discuss initiatives and strategies for promoting financial literacy, ensuring individuals have the knowledge to make informed financial decisions.**

INCLUSIVE FINANCE: **Explore the role of finance in promoting inclusive economic growth. Discuss how financial institutions can contribute to bridging the gap and providing financial services to underserved communities, fostering economic inclusion.**

SUSTAINABLE PRACTICES IN FINANCE

GREEN FINANCE INITIATIVES

ECO-FRIENDLY INVESTMENTS: **Delve into the realm of green finance and environmentally conscious investments. Explore how sustainable practices contribute to mitigating climate change and building a more resilient and responsible financial ecosystem.**

CIRCULAR ECONOMY PRINCIPLES:
Discuss the principles of the circular economy in finance. Explore how adopting circular economy practices can reduce waste, promote resource efficiency, and contribute to sustainable economic development.

THE FUTURE OF FINANCE WITH A HUMAN TOUCH

HUMAN-CENTRIC TECHNOLOGICAL INTEGRATION

ROBO-ADVISORS AND HUMAN OVERSIGHT:**Examine the integration of robo-advisors in financial services. Discuss the importance of maintaining human oversight to ensure ethical and responsible use of technology in financial decision-making.**

CUSTOMER-CENTRIC INNOVATION: **Explore innovations that prioritise the needs of customers. Discuss how financial institutions can leverage technology to enhance customer experience while upholding ethical standards and human values.**

CRAFTING A HUMAN-CENTRIC FINANCIAL FUTURE
As we conclude this chapter, you're equipped with a holistic understanding of the human element in finance. Navigate the intricacies of emotional intelligence, ethical considerations, financial education, sustainability, and the integration of human-centric values in the future of finance. Your journey towards a responsible and human-centric financial future is marked by empathy, integrity, and a commitment to the well-being of individuals and communities.